BIBLICAL COUNSELING AND

COMMON
GRACE

CRITICAL ISSUES IN BIBLICAL COUNSELING

BIBLICAL COUNSELING AND

COMMON GRACE

HEATH LAMBERT

Common grace is not a license, nor does it belong in the rubbish bin. Lambert provides the biblical balance needed on this topic as it relates to the care of souls. Through a wonderfully woven case study, he guides the reader with clarity to consider the counseling implications of consequential truths. You will see why biblical and theological precision are critical to the practice of counseling care.

DR. DALE JOHNSON,
Executive Director of The Association of Certified Biblical Counselors; Director of counseling programs and Associate Professor of Biblical Counseling at Midwestern Baptist Theological Seminary

Heath Lambert has written a concise and persuasive call to fully embrace biblical authority and sufficiency in our personal practice of "one another" ministry. This book is an important contribution to the contemporary conversation as well as essential reading for pastors, counselors, and ministry leaders.

PAUL TAUTGES,
Pastor and author of *Remade: Embracing Your Complete Identity in Christ, Anxiety: Knowing God's Peace, Counseling One Another,* and many others

If you ever doubted whether or not God's Word is sufficient to counsel the experience of traumatic circumstances, this book is a must read. In it, Lambert weaves throughout the story of a very troubled young lady while showing how insufficient and destructive it is to combine God's Word with current psychological trends in trauma care. At the same time, there is real and lasting hope employed using Psalm 107 (as an example), which clearly unfolds the effectiveness and sufficiency of God's Word for the traumatized and deeply hurting.

This seasoned pastor and counselor addresses the fallacies of popular Christian counselors whose approach supposes God's Word insufficient to meet serious counseling needs. He explains well the dangers of waving the "common-grace-needed" flag, out of a misunderstanding of common grace and its limitations in counseling. In short, what has been given to us is a very readable apologetic on the sufficiency of Scripture in the counseling arena, when employed with an abundance of grace and applicable Truth. Every believer can benefit from this book, but especially those who desire to minister effectively to those touched by trauma and struggling with its effects.

DR. STUART SCOTT,
Director of Membership Services and a Professor of Biblical
Counseling at The Master's University in Santa Clarita, CA;
Director of the Center for Biblical Counseling at Bob Jones
University; Professor of Biblical Counseling at BJU Seminary

❖

Biblical Counseling and Common Grace
Heath Lambert

Copyright © 2023, Heath Lambert

ISBNS:
Paper: 978-1-63342-321-3
ePub: 978-1-63342-322-0

Cover design and typeset by www.greatwriting.org

Printed in Colombia

Shepherd Press
P.O. Box 24
Wapwallopen, PA 18660
www.shepherdpress.com

The Critical Issues in Biblical Counseling resources cherish and foster a defining and discerning view of biblical counseling faithful to the founders of the Biblical Counseling Movement. Intentionally embracing an historical, biblical-counseling, sufficiency-of-Scripture model, CIBC books

- Address current and emerging issues with robust biblical and doctrinal clarity, showing the beautiful wisdom of Scripture;
- Assert a truth paradigm for the future generations of biblical counselors;
- Announce a warning against biblically inconsistent, weak, or erroneous teachings;
- Advance biblical-counseling thinking within the parameters of an historic sufficiency-of-Scripture model;
- Arm readers with a clarifying lens to grow in discernment;
- Aim for the exaltation of Christ, and clearly proclaim the power of the gospel and Scripture to address the most difficult issues of life,

in order that counselors and counselees will
live lives of consistent worship for
the glory of God.

To Mammaw
Whose love and uncommon grace saved my life

A Word from the Consulting Editor

Biblical counseling has been a huge blessing in my life. In the 1970s, I began to learn about the practical and powerful nature of Scripture. My life was radically transformed as I began to take the Bible seriously. In particular, Ephesians 4 was used by the Lord in a very precise way in my life to help me deal with bitterness and to seek to reconcile a broken relationship. It was wonderful to learn that Jay Adams was applying the doctrines of inspiration, inerrancy and the sufficiency of Scripture to the counseling room.

By the grace of God, I was then able to study under David Powlison, Edward Welch, and Paul Tripp. They taught me about the worshiping nature of my heart, and how humans have a disposition to false worship. I realized that we do not just have some type of unquantifiable brain disorder, we have worship disorders. I went back to school to learn how to help others, but the Lord used the classes in significant ways to counsel me. It was refreshing to experience a deeper growth in my relationship with the Lord.

Through the years, by the grace of God, I have seen countless lives transformed by the Word of God as it is applied to life. Mediations have taken place in relationships which were seemingly hopeless, and these relationships have been reconciled. Precious people have come to faith in Christ. The chains of horrible addictions have been broken. Marriages have been restored.

I am writing this because I want you, the reader, to be blessed as well. It is my desire for you to experience the sanctifying power of the Word of God and for you to be confident that Scripture is an inexhaustible well of wisdom to be applied in practical ways to those struggling with personal problems. However, there is a concern.

We all feel the intensity of the days in which we are living. We are in a new era. New solutions to human problems are being proposed, and this is raising new questions. What is the role of common grace in using extrabiblical resources? Is historic biblical counseling opposed to science? Out of love, shouldn't we use secular methodologies to help people? How should we, as biblical counselors, think about using the *The Diagnostic and Statistical Manual* (DSM)? How should biblical counselors apply the findings of neuroscience? How do we help those who are confused about their gender? What is the role of a biblical counselor? Should biblical counselors deal with cases of trauma?

This series, *Critical Issues in Biblical Counseling,* is being written with the concern that some of the answers being proposed in the broader biblical-counseling world are inaccurate and are leading historic biblical counseling down a path that will undermine the sufficiency of Scripture. It is also being written with the conviction that Scripture, accurately interpreted and creatively and properly applied, has answers for the deepest human struggles.

In this book, Heath Lambert addresses the important topic of the doctrine of common grace. He exhibits a command of the subject and with laserlike precision demonstrates the beauties and limitations of this crucial doctrine. He also emphasizes what historic biblical counseling has taught concerning the sufficiency of Scripture, and he shows the weaknesses of endeavoring to use the doctrine of common grace to allow for integration of secular methodologies. Of course, this is all for the glory of God and the good of His people through the power of the gospel.

DR. ERNIE BAKER
CIBC Consulting Editor

1

Common Grace
and Truth

A book called *Biblical Counseling and Common Grace* might seem to hold little relevance to all but a few with the most obscure interests. "I'd read a book like that," I hear you saying, "if I had a specific interest in understanding the doctrine of common grace or if I were interested in the discipline of counseling. Without that, I would rather read a book more relevant to my life."

If a statement like that resonates with you, I would like the opportunity to persuade you that this is a book you *need* to read. This little book about counseling and common grace has everything to do with the lives most of us are living. I want to prove this to you by telling you the story of a precious woman I know. I will call her Julia.

Julia's Story

I first noticed Julia standing nervously off to the side near the front of our auditorium after church. That place down front is where I linger each week at the conclusion of our service to pray, encourage, answer questions, and even take pictures. I could see Julia watching from a distance, trying to decide if she would join the crowd of people laughing and talking. I decided to make it easy on her and, as soon as I could, walked over and introduced myself.

She told me her name and how she had recently started attending our church. I could tell she was apprehensive, and so I tried to navigate the situation carefully, giving enough attention to let her know I was interested in her without making her feel she had to hang around longer than she felt comfortable. After a moment or two of light conversation, she clutched her Bible close to her chest and, without explanation, thanked me. Then she turned and walked away.

Over the next few weeks, I came to know more of Julia's story. She had started to attend our church, participate in Sunday School, and was getting connected in several relationships. She started to come down front after church more regularly and began to feel increasingly comfortable talking with me and my wife. As we got to know her, she began to share a tragic story that broke our hearts. She grew up in a very religious home with a dad who served as a pastor and with a very faithful mom. The problem was that her pastor-father was also an incredibly wicked man. He was physically abusive to her mom and sexually abusive to her.

Julia's entire childhood centered around living with a man who sexually abused her during the week and preached to her from the church's pulpit every Sunday. She came to our church a broken and confused woman. She had monumental questions that plagued her: what kind of religion creates predators who preach? Is anyone who they say they are? Is any man safe? Can I ever overcome the feelings of terror I've carried for decades and live a normal, happy life?

This book is about Julia. It is also about how to

help her and others like her. This is a book about what to say to help her turn the corner and live a life of faith, hope, love, peace, and joy. If you are one of the Julias in the world, or if you are called to help someone like her, I want to explain why common grace has *everything* to do with you.

The Doctrine of Common Grace

Protestants believe that grace comes from God in two wide streams. The most important of these streams is referred to as special grace. Special grace refers to all the particular workings of God in individual lives where the eyes of lost and sinful people are opened to see the light of the gospel of the glory of Christ (2 Cor. 4:4-6), where they are regenerated with new hearts (Ezek. 36:24-27), justified (Rom. 3:23-24), adopted (Rom. 8:14-15), and, ultimately fully sanctified (1 Thess. 5:23-24)—all as a result of the life, death, and resurrection of Jesus Christ. Special grace is, therefore, the grace of God that comes uniquely to His people out of all the sinful mass of humanity in the world. But this glorious stream of grace is not the only one available in God's world.

Common grace is the other stream of grace and refers to the good kindness of God that He shows to all people regardless of whether they have experienced the salvation that comes through Jesus Christ alone.[1] It is a doctrine deeply rooted in the Protestant Reformation. John Calvin has been credited as the primary person who recovered the doctrine, but

1 Heath Lambert, *A Theology of Biblical Counseling: The Doctrinal Foundations of Counseling Ministry* (Grand Rapids, MI: Zondervan, 2016), 67. This is the definition of common grace that I use in my chapter on the topic.

other influential theologians like Abraham Kuyper, Herman Bavinck, and Cornelius Van Til have followed in his footsteps.[2]

The doctrine of common grace solves an important dilemma created by the existence of two other truths. The first truth is the reality of the comprehensive and catastrophic implications of sin in the lives of fallen humanity. The apostle Paul leaves no room for human righteousness when he announces in Romans 3:10–18:

> None is righteous, no, not one; no one under-
> stands; no one seeks for God. All have turned
> aside; together they have become worthless;
> no one does good, not even one. Their throat
> is an open grave; they use their tongues to de-
> ceive. The venom of asps is under their lips.
> Their mouth is full of curses and bitterness.
> Their feet are swift to shed blood; in their paths
> are ruin and misery, and the way of peace they
> have not known. There is no fear of God before
> their eyes.

Calvin reflects on this biblical reality when he says, "Man has no remaining good in himself, and is beset on every side by the most miserable destitution."[3] To those who would speak contrary to this biblical position and attempt to advocate for

2 See Herman Bavinck, "Common Grace," *Calvin Theological Journal,* (Grand Rapids, MI: Calvin Theological Seminary, 1989), 51. Herman Bavinck credits Calvin as the one primarily responsible for developing the doctrine that Bavinck himself referred to as common grace.

3 John Calvin, *Institutes of the Christian Religion* (Grand Rapids, MI: Eerdmans, 1989), 2.2.1, 223.

the presence of some goodness in fallen humanity, Calvin adds, "Those who invest us with more than we possess only add sacrilege to our ruin."[4] So, one obvious truth creating the dilemma which leads us to the doctrine of common grace is the clarity of Protestant theology on the biblical teaching of the sinfulness of humanity.

The second truth leading to a need for the doctrine of common grace is the obvious good we see throughout the world. Though humanity has been devasted by sin, and though that sin produces effects that utterly shake the cosmos (cf. Rom. 8:20–22), we still see much good in people and in the world around us. In the sphere of government, we are aware of examples of human beings governing with righteousness in this sinful world. In the sphere of society, there are many communities living together in beauty, joy, and harmony. The world of the arts produces everything from Mozart's Concerto No 21 in C Major to The Mona Lisa to Dickens's *Great Expectations*. In the arena of medicine, we live in a remarkable world of penicillin, painkillers, and pacemakers—just to name a few modern marvels.

The goodness seen in the world is not merely a product of observation but is also founded on clear biblical teaching. Psalm 145:9 says, "The LORD is good to all, and his mercy is over all that he has made." Inspired by the Holy Spirit, David makes clear that the goodness of God ensures that we live in a remarkable world full of blessing, goodness, and grace.

Protestant theologians have refused to reject the goodness in creation that is observed by all and

4 Ibid.

taught in Scripture. Calvin believed such a rejection to be nearly insane:

> How, then, can we deny that truth must have beamed on those ancient lawgivers who arranged civil order and discipline with so much equity? Shall we say that the philosophers, in their exquisite researches and skillful description of nature, were blind? Shall we deny the possession of intellect to those who drew up rules for discourse, and taught us to speak in accordance with reason? Shall we say that those who by cultivation of the medical art, expended their industry in our behalf were only raving? What shall we say of the mathematical sciences? Shall we deem them to be the dreams of madmen? Nay, we cannot read the writings of the ancients on these subjects without the highest admiration; an admiration which their excellence will not allow us to withhold."[5]

Bavinck follows Calvin in acknowledging the contributions of unbelievers, "It would not do to deny the true, the good, and the beautiful that one can see in mankind outside of Christ. That would not only be in conflict with experience but would also entail a denial of God's gifts and hence constitute ingratitude toward him."[6] A rejection of the goodness of God in creation is a denial of our experience and of God's own Word.

The existence of fallen humanity, together with the obvious good in the world, are two competing

5 Ibid., 2.2.15, 236.
6 See Bavinck, "Common Grace," *Calvin Theological Journal*, 51.

facts that create a significant theological dilemma. How can human beings be sinful to the core and yet capable of the kinds of wondrous good we see in life and are taught in the Bible? To ask the question another way, "How is it that men who still lie under the wrath and curse of God and are heirs of hell enjoy so many good gifts at the hand of God?"[7]

The biblical solution to this dilemma is found in a proper theology of common grace. The Bible teaches that the horrible sinfulness of humanity does not change the disposition of God to be gracious even to those who do not know Him through faith in Jesus Christ.[8] Instead, God is kind to the entire world—both to those who know Him by faith, and to those who persist in unbelief. The reason for any goodness in a sinful world is owing to the grace of God, which He commonly bestows on the entire world.

Protestant theology has found many ways to express the gifts we receive in the common grace of God.[9] The most typical way of discussing the gifts of

7 John Murray, "Common Grace" in *Collected Writings of John Murray*, vol. 2 (Edinburgh: Banner of Truth, 1982), 93.

8 This statement is actually quite controversial in historic discussions on common grace. Some, like Herman Hoeksema, have argued that it is impossible for God to have a kind disposition to objects of His wrath. Cornelius Van Til, who disagrees with Hoeksema, calls this theological argument the common grace problem. This debate is important, but, in a book of this size, we will not be able to enter these waters. In this book, we will assume the existence of common grace based on the overwhelming weight of biblical evidence evaluated below. In these pages, we will focus on the reality of common grace and how to apply it to counseling. Arguments responding to the claim that it does not exist are outside the scope of this work.

9 Previously, I have discussed three separate categories of common grace: divine moral provision, divine physical provision, and divine intellectual provision. See Lambert, *A Theology of Biblical Counseling*, 67-70.

common grace has to do with the ideas of restraining and bestowing. God's common grace is seen in the bad things He withholds and the good things He gives.

Negatively, God's common grace comes to this lost world by restraining the effects of its sin. Many examples exist of this in Scripture, including the mark God placed on Cain to protect him from harm (Gen. 4:15), the creation of many languages, and the dispersion of people at Babel to prevent them from exalting themselves above God (Gen. 11:6-8), God's work to prohibit Abimelech from sin (Gen. 20:6), God's writing of the law on the hearts of unregenerate people (Rom. 2:14-15), and the divine restraint of the man of lawlessness (2 Thess. 2:7). Human beings regularly fail to give full vent to the sin dwelling deep in their soul. Such failures do not trace back to any goodness in man but to the common grace of God that restrains sin.

Positively, God's common grace is demonstrated by giving humanity all the wonderful things needed to live life on earth. Clear thinking is possible because of God's common grace illumining our minds (John 1:9). Rain, sunshine, and fruitful crops giving us everything we need to live life is also a result of the common grace of God (Ps. 65:9-13; 104:10-15, 27-30; 136:25; 145:15-16; Matt. 5:45). More than that, these wonderful gifts are not provided merely to bless us, but also to leave a witness testifying to the good existence of God (cf., Acts 14:16-17; Rom. 2:4).

Common grace does not just grant gifts to people but teaches them an important lesson about the character of God. We learn this lesson in the Sermon on the Mount:

But I say to you, Love your enemies and pray for those who persecute you, so that you may be sons of your Father who is in heaven. For he makes his sun rise on the evil and on the good, and sends rain on the just and on the unjust. For if you love those who love you, what reward do you have? Do not even the tax collectors do the same? And if you greet only your brothers, what more are you doing than others? Do not even the Gentiles do the same? You therefore must be perfect, as your heavenly Father is perfect (Matt. 5:44-48).

Jesus teaches the truth of common grace when He makes clear that God makes the sun rise and the rain fall on those who love Him as well as those who hate Him. His teaching clarifies that redemption is not required in order to receive temporal blessings from God. This teaching on common grace, however, does not stand alone but is the theological foundation for the command Jesus gives to us to love our enemies. We are supposed to love our enemies because of God's love for His enemies, and when we follow this command, we will be perfect as our heavenly Father is perfect. Christians, of course, cannot love their enemies as they should and so will not be perfect in this life. But God does love His enemies and is perfect. That means common grace does not just give us the things we need, but is also evidence of God's very own perfection.

Responding to Common Grace

When we understand the truth of common grace, we will respond appropriately to it. For Calvin, there are two necessary ways to react to the doctrine. The first response is gratitude. Calvin says, "If we reflect that the Spirit of God is the only fountain of truth, we will be careful, as we would avoid offering insult to him, not to reject or condemn truth wherever it appears. In despising the gifts, we insult the Giver."[10] For Calvin, an awareness of the common grace of God will make Christians grateful. If we ungratefully reject the good gifts of God in this fallen world, we sin by insulting His holy name.

The second response to common grace is to use the good things that God gives to us. Once again, Calvin says, "But if the Lord has been pleased to assist us by the work and ministry of the ungodly in physics, dialectics, mathematics, and other similar sciences, let us avail ourselves of it, lest, by neglecting the gifts of God spontaneously offered to us, we be justly punished for our sloth."[11] It is important that Calvin refers to the work of the "ungodly" in their various disciplines of physics, dialectics, mathematics, and all the rest as their "ministry." He says this ministry exists to "assist" Christians and that if we reject it, we are guilty of sloth. Calvin indicts Christians who reject the fruit of common grace as lazy.

Common grace guarantees that we will experience tremendous good in this broken world. Farmers will develop ways to grow enough wheat to feed billions of people, surgeons can access a cocktail of drugs to put

10 Calvin, *Institutes of the Christian Religion*, 2.2.15, 236.
11 Ibid., 2.2.16, 236-37.

you into a deep sleep so you do not feel it when they cut into your brain, engineers erect buildings that are hundreds of stories high, educators create learning strategies for disabled students, chefs prepare fish with spicy mango salsa, musicians write captivating music, technologists develop digital systems that purvey that music out to the entire world, and ten trillion other things besides all this. Our sin makes this world hard, but common grace ensures that it is also wonderful.

Common grace ought to overwhelm us with the manifold kindness of God that He gives to undeserving sinners. Every good thing we experience, from ravioli to the relief of pain, is an occasion for us to worship God and remember that "Every good gift and every perfect gift is from above, coming down from the Father of lights" (James 1:17).

2

Common Grace
and Sin

Julia, the young woman I met and began to know in the front of our auditorium after church one Sunday, has an absolutely tragic story. No compassionate person will be uninterested in helping her. But what do you do? What do you say? Where will you find the resources to know how to start?

If we are honest, most people in our world today would resort to a Google search. The bad news about such a search is that it will yield an impossible number of resources you might try (my own search led to 120,000,000 results!). It's worse than that. When you try and examine these resources, you discover that there are almost as many different approaches to understanding and relieving Julia's problems as there are resources themselves. How are we supposed to know where to start with so many different perspectives?

Let me make a start by reducing the number of results from 120,000,000 down to two. We will start with two famous and influential books that came up in my search on the topic. One book is an old bestseller called *The Power of Positive Thinking* by Norman Vincent Peale.[12]

If you choose Peale's book, as many have before you, you will lead Julia on a path to creating strong

12 Norman Vincent Peale, *The Power of Positive Thinking* (New York, NY: Touchstone, 1952).

visions of triumph to drown out the thoughts of pain from her past. You will guide her to frame her own picture of victory and imagine herself succeeding until she reaches her ideal. So, you could begin a journey with Julia that starts her on the path to positive thinking. That's one option.

Another option that showed up in my search is relatively new. It is *The Body Keeps the Score* by Bessel van der Kolk.[13] This book is another bestseller but is much more recent than Peale's. If you choose to take the path charted by van der Kolk, you and Julia will begin a journey that takes you on fascinating discoveries of neuroscience. You will be taught that the kind of trauma Julia has experienced is written onto her brain, and dealing with that trauma requires a number of interventions, from breathing techniques to eye exercises known as eye movement desensitization and reprocessing.

The thinking of these two authors is very different. The approaches their books commend are, therefore, also quite different. And these are just two books. Were we to continue to sift through Google's results, we would encounter a dizzying array of options. How are we to know which of the numerous paths to take in helping Julia? Another question, very relevant to this book, is whether an understanding of common grace can help us in knowing what to choose?

The doctrine of common grace does have a lot to teach about which resources to use in helping Julia, but we need to say more. In order to see the relevance of the doctrine of common grace for counseling, we

13 Bessel van der Kolk, *The Body Keeps the Score* (New York, NY: Penguin Random House, 2014).

need to understand the reality of another doctrine that exists in tension with common grace.

Common Grace and the Corrosive Effects of Sin

So far, we have seen that the doctrine of common grace is an abundantly biblical doctrine that resolves the tension created by the comprehensive sinfulness of humanity on the one hand and people's ability to do good things on the other. We have seen that this doctrine should result in Christians utilizing the fruit of common grace whenever they receive it and should inspire thankfulness for the products of common grace. We have seen, that is to say, a very positive perspective on the work that comes from unbelievers in this fallen world.

Common grace, however, is not the only factor that defines what people do in a sinful world. To understand the other reality, we must remember that, in terms of logical development, the Protestant understanding of common grace follows an understanding of the sinfulness of humanity. As I have observed, the doctrine of common grace explains how so much good exists in a world with people who are so sinful. We cannot understand the common grace of God until we understand the sinfulness of humanity.

Earlier, we read a description from the apostle Paul about the devasting reality of sinful human behavior. Now, we must consider a devastating description of sinful human thinking: "They are darkened in their understanding, alienated from the life of God because of the ignorance that is in them, due to their hardness of heart" (Eph. 4:18). The human mind is darkened, and people are ignorant because of the hardening impact of sin on their thinking. Calvin's teaching reflects this biblical perspective:

> In the perverted and degenerate nature of man there are still some sparks which show that he is a rational animal, and differs from the brutes, inasmuch as he is endued with intelligence, and yet, that this light is so smothered by clouds of darkness, that it cannot shine forth to any good effect.[14]

Elsewhere he makes clear that once sin has done its work on the mind of sinful man, "A shapeless ruin is all that remains."[15] He furthermore makes clear that these devastating consequences are not accidental but intentional on the part of sinful people who, "Intentionally stupefy themselves."[16]

Theologians refer to the stupefying impact of sin on our thinking as the noetic effects of sin. The word "noetic" comes from the Greek word, *nous,* and is a reference to the impact of sin on our minds. The impact of sin on our minds must be evaluated in any consideration of common grace. It is important to make several early observations.

14 John Calvin, *Institutes of the Christian Religion*, 2.2.12, 233.
15 Ibid., 2.2.12, 233.
16 Ibid.,1.4.2, 47.

Common Grace and
Noetic Effects: Implications

First, without taking away any of our gratitude for all the blessings we experience in this sinful world, we must also make clear that the biblical teaching on the noetic effects of sin means that common grace does not remove the fundamental sinfulness of humanity. Bavinck says,

> Since after the fall people have remained human and continue to share in the blessings of God's common grace, they can inwardly possess many virtues and outwardly do many good deeds that, viewed through man's eyes and measured by human standards, are greatly to be appreciated and of great value for human life. But this is not to say that they are good in the eyes of God and correspond to the full spiritual sense of his holy law.[17]

Common grace is a remarkable kindness of God to allow human beings the capacity for good, but this kindness neither reverses nor removes the fundamental fallenness of sinful people. It is only the work of God's special saving grace that reverses the corrosive effects of sin. And that reversal for God's people is only partial in this life. The full removal of the devastating consequences of sin awaits the end of history and the new heavens and the new earth.

17 Herman Bavinck, *Reformed Dogmatics: Holy Spirit, Church, and New Creation,* vol. 4 (Grand Rapids, MI: Baker Academic, 2008), 256-57. Also see Calvin, *Institutes of the Christian Religion,* 2.2.12.

Second, the tension created by the coexistence of common grace and the noetic effects of sin means the thinking, discoveries, and products of sinful humanity will be mixed. A world full of common grace *and* the noetic effects of sin will be complicated. James talks about the strange reality where the same mouth produces blessings and cursings (James 3:10). We see this same strange reality at work in a world where common grace can produce something as wonderful as the Internet, but the effects of sin can fill it up with pornography. In God's common grace, we live in a world with amazing medical achievements, but because of the noetic effects of sin, one physician botches a surgery that another can accomplish with ease. We are able to build majestic bridges from the fruit of common grace, but the noetic effects of sin will lead to engineering errors that cause them to collapse. A world full of common grace and the noetic effects of sin mean we live in a world that is a mixed bag of wonder and woe.

Third, because we live in a world where the noetic effects of sin remain in spite of God's common grace, this means that common grace is not a guarantee that any particular thought, discovery, or product of anyone is necessarily correct. The existence of common grace is not an argument for the correctness of anything in particular. This reality is specifically important in considering the recent trend on the part of some counselors to encourage the general embrace of secular approaches to counseling based on the mere existence of common grace.[18] An

18 For an example of this see Nate Brooks, "Herman Bavinck, Patron Saint of Biblical Counselors: How an Old Dutch Theologian Helps Us Make Sense of Biblical Sufficiency," accessed July 27, 2023, https://rts.edu/resources/herman-bavinck-pa-

uncritical race to embrace secular theories based on a simplistic acceptance of common grace is the exact kind of intellectual laziness we would expect as a result of the noetic effects of sin.

Fourth, the coexistence of common grace together with the noetic effects of sin requires thoughtful Christians to evaluate the thinking, discoveries, and products of all people with great theological care. A simplistic evaluation of the created order based in undue optimism would simply embrace everything the world has to offer under the enthusiastic banner of common grace. A simplistic evaluation of the created order based in undue pessimism simply rejects everything the world has to offer under the suspicious banner of the noetic effects of sin. Careful Christians embracing the entire Bible will approach the created order with care in a desire to embrace everything that rightly exists under the banner of common grace and to reject anything that is the product of the power of sin.

A final observation we can make about the implication of the noetic effects of sin and the existence of common grace has to do with the earthly and heavenly or the worldly and the spiritual. Calvin elaborates:

> We have one kind of intelligence of earth-
> ly things, and another of heavenly things. By
> earthly things, I mean those which are related
> not to God and his kingdom, to true righteous-
> ness and future blessedness, but have some

tron-saint-of-biblical-counselors/. In this address, Brooks makes much of a doctrine of common grace, which we are right to embrace. His enthusiasm about the doctrine of common grace, however, is not appropriately nuanced by a biblical understanding of the noetic effects of sin.

> connection with the present life, and are in a manner confined within its boundaries. By heavenly things, I mean the pure knowledge of God, the method of true righteousness, and the mysteries of the heavenly kingdom. To the former belong matters of policy and economy, all mechanical arts and liberal studies. To the latter . . . belong the knowledge of God and of his will, and the means of framing the life in accordance with them.[19]

Basic to a Protestant understanding of the doctrine of common grace are the two planes on which it operates. Reformation theologians make a distinction between the earthly plane and the heavenly, the physical and the spiritual, or the higher and the lower order. The earthly plane has to do with matters of this life and the present physical world in which we live. It is sometimes understood as the lower order of things. This lower order has to do with the development of vaccinations, with architectural engineering, with complex navigation equipment on airplanes, filing systems at your local library, and things like this. The fruit of God's common grace is most obvious in this lower order.

It is here in this lower order that there is a debate among Protestant theologians who admit the existence of common grace. Kuyper and Bavinck not only did much to develop the thinking of Calvin, but they have also been accused of departing from it in an important way. The argument is that they were correct in seeing

19 Calvin, *Institutes of the Christian Religion*, 2.2.13, 234; See also Cornelius Van Til, *Common Grace and the Gospel* (Phillipsburg, NJ: P&R Publishing, 2015), 23; Louis Berkhof, *Systematic Theology*, (Grand Rapids, MI: Eerdmans, 1932), 440.

the operations of common grace but too frequently lost the balance of the noetic effects of sin and so became too optimistic about the fruit of common grace in this area.[20] Van Til believed he shared the same basic theological position as these men, but also was concerned for them to remember that

> There is no sinner who, unless regenerated, does not actually seek to interpret himself and the universe without God. The natural man uses his logical powers to describe the facts of creation as though these facts existed apart from God.[21]

In the faithful line of Protestant theologians embracing common grace, Van Til claims a distinction between Calvin and himself on the one hand, and Kuyper and Bavinck on the other. According to Van Til, Kuyper and Bavinck could be guilty of emphasizing common grace to the exclusion of the noetic effects of sin in the lower order. This reality is one we will need to remember as we witness an instinct toward this same overemphasis in our day.

The best way to talk about the reality of sin and grace in the lower order of things is to make clear that the noetic effects of sin remain damagingly present in this lower order, but not in such a way that lost individuals can make no true observations or discoveries.

This lower order is not the only level that exists. The higher order of things has to do with the reality

20 For more information on why Van Til believed Kuyper and Bavinck had departed from a consistently Reformed view of common grace see Van Til, *Common Grace and the Gospel*, 45-72.

21 Ibid., 55.

of the heavenly or spiritual realm. This higher order involves the existence and nature of God, the sacred teachings of the Bible, the nature of who people are, the purpose of what it means to be alive, who Jesus is, how to get to heaven, and things like this. In this realm of special grace, common grace does not get us very far at all. The noetic effects of sin attack the core essence of what it means to have any kind of understanding at this level. The Bible makes clear that this is because a person must be informed by the Spirit to understand spiritual things. "The natural person does not accept the things of the Spirit of God, for they are folly to him, and he is not able to understand them because they are spiritually discerned" (1 Cor. 2:14; cf. Rom. 1:18, 21-23).

Common Grace and Noetic Effects: Evaluation

The complexity of living in a sinful world where God, nevertheless, showers His blessings on all mankind creates the need for Christians to think in careful ways. How are Christians to know what thinking, discoveries, and products are defined by a greater degree of common grace and which ones are defined by a greater degree of the noetic effects of sin? It is possible to answer this question with a threefold level of analysis.

One of the obvious signs of the aging process in my life is the constant deterioration of my eyesight. For several years now, my annual visit to the optometrist has resulted in an ever-stronger prescription for glasses. Then, last year, the optometrist really let me have it. He told me it was time for bifocals.

The idea behind bifocals is that clear sight requires one prescription to see further distances and another prescription to see up close. I take some comfort in knowing my condition is not as bad as the consulting editor of this book series who needs trifocals, which require still another prescription to see midrange. Such corrective eyewear is not only a demonstration of common grace, but also shows that sometimes we need multiple lenses to see things clearly. In evaluating whether the thinking, discoveries, and products of people are the result of common grace, the noetic effects of sin, or some combination, it is necessary to utilize three lenses.

The Lens of Assumption

The first lens we must use to evaluate the presence of common grace is the lens of assumption. We use this lens to look at the world and assume the presence of common grace. The assumption of common grace is grounded experientially and theologically. Experientially, we see God's common grace everywhere. In God's kindness, I am writing these words a few weeks after my sixth brain surgery, where a room full of remarkably skilled neurosurgeons performed work beneath my skull that prior generations could not imagine. I write these words on a very sophisticated piece of technology and am able to see these words through a helpful pair of glasses. The grace to make my laptop and my glasses did not require that the experts were Christians. As I write, I am preparing to go on a date with my wife to celebrate our anniversary. We made reservations for the restaurant on a phone system that is a communications marvel.

We selected a restaurant for dinner based solely on our expectation for excellent food, not whether the people making it are believers or not. Every moment of every day, we are all living in a glorious world, experiencing glorious blessings from the glorious hand of God Himself.

More importantly, the lens of assumption has a theological grounding. The Bible itself teaches us that God loves us and gives us gifts to enjoy simply because we are members of the human race and irrespective of whether we are saved. The promise of James 1:17 that "Every good gift and every perfect gift is from above, coming down from the Father" is true for all people, whether Christian or not. Calvin referred to the obvious nature of the "many gifts the Lord has left in possession of human nature" by saying these gifts were "manifest."[22]

The lens of assumption is something far richer than assuming that life will be easy and wonderful. The lens of assumption is about trusting in the great love of God, believing in Him, and having confidence that when He says He will provide the world with good things, it is true. These words are not just a description of life, they are a promise from God to His people. We can assume it is true.

The Lens of Analysis

But things get more complicated. In a world full of the common grace of God, we can assume that we will benefit from many wonderful things. However, the noetic effects of sin make many of those wonderful benefits hard to discern. The corrupting power

22 Calvin, *Institutes of the Christian Religion*, 2.2.15, 236.

of sin means discerning what is good, bad, true, and false is far more difficult than we care to admit and much more complex than an easy embrace of common grace would allow. Disagreements among experts, ignorance of crucial information, and even a staunch commitment to error all play a part in making it difficult to discern between a matter defined by common grace or the noetic effects of sin. When this difficulty occurs, as it regularly does, we need more than the lens of assumption. We need the lens of analysis. Let me describe the lens of analysis to you in very personal terms.

As I write, I am under the care of numerous physicians after years of difficulty and six significant operations. The difficulty started in 2017 with small twitches on the right side of my body. Ultimately, these twitches became spasms that caused my face to scrunch up tightly with increasing frequency. When these spasms would happen, I could not open my eyes, talk, chew, or drink. For a man who likes to see, talk, and eat, these problems were far more than an inconvenience. In God's common grace, I met with the finest neurosurgeons available and discovered that the problem had to do with a tiny nerve in my brain about the size of the lead from a mechanical pencil. A cluster of nearby blood vessels had come to rest on that nerve compressing it and causing all the problems. My surgeries have mostly been to relocate those blood vessels and to relieve the pressure on the nerve.

The story of how neurosurgeons came to that knowledge is a fascinating one. Physicians have known about problems like mine for centuries but have not known what caused them or how to treat them. Then, in the 1960s, a resident in neurosurgery named Peter Janetta was dissecting a set of cranial nerves when he noticed something amazing—a tiny blood vessel was resting on one of the cranial nerves and had made a deep indentation in it. He went to his professors and said he thought this could be the cause of the nerve problem that had plagued so many for so long. They dismissed what he said. They believed there was no way such a big problem could be rooted in something so tiny. Janetta waved off their rejection and devoted himself to the study and cure of this problem. Today, the surgery he developed called microvascular decompression, or the Janetta Procedure, cures thousands of people a year afflicted with this debilitating problem.[23]

The point of this story is that very smart, highly trained people disagreed for a long time about what was true and what was false. Janetta thought he had found the truth in tiny blood vessels compressing the cranial nerve. Others with more experience than Janetta thought there was no way this was possible. So, was Janetta's theory the product of common grace or the noetic effects of sin? This question was a complicated and highly technical one to answer. We now know Janetta's discovery was defined by common grace. But it took the lens of analysis used over years by highly trained people to figure it out.

This is only one example. In this complicated world, we cannot always assume we have encountered common grace. The lens of analysis is required every

23 For a brief survey of this story see Margalit Fox, "Dr. Peter J. Jannetta, Pioneering Neurosurgeon on Facial Pain, Dies at 84," accessed on July 26, 2023, https://www.nytimes.com/2016/04/15/science/dr-peter-j-jannetta-a-pioneer-in-neurosurgery-dies-at-84.html.

day to discover what is true, right, and good. Should our diets be low in carbohydrates or low in calories? Is global warming a true reality? If it is, is it caused by human behavior or natural cycles in the weather? Which political candidate holds the most promise for running the government in your city, state, or country? Which mechanic is telling the truth about what it would take to fix your car? Which history book is telling the truth about the American Revolution? Even when we have strong answers to these questions, we can find just as many other people with the opposite answers. Living life in this mixed-up world often requires far more than a theoretical embrace of common grace and the noetic effects of sin. It can take years of hard work, patient study, and careful research.

The Lens of Authority

In telling the difference between common grace and the noetic effects of sin, much of the time, using the lens of assumption, we can simply take common grace for granted. Most of us do not require a lengthy investigative procedure to receive the gifts of lunch, air conditioning, medical care, or the hugs of a loved one. We do, however, regularly encounter things more challenging and complex that move us from assumption to analysis. Regularly, we need to carefully analyze difficult matters over long periods of time and with the help of people far more expert than we are. And then, at other times, we need the lens of biblical authority.

The doctrine of biblical authority means that Scripture has the ultimate and final word over everything that it teaches. In practical terms, this teaching requires us to embrace the Bible as true and submit to everything God teaches in His Word. The faithful Christian knows that regardless of how many experts debate something, no position can be characterized by common grace if it stands in violation of God's Word.

Many issues serve as examples of this fact. Highly educated professionals advocate for the so-called medical right to an abortion for any and every reason. Though the Bible is not a medical manual, it still speaks authoritatively into the practice of medicine and forbids the practice of abortion with its teaching on the value of human life (cf. Gen. 1:27; Ex. 20:13; Ps. 139:13-16). Many men and women with their PhDs in geology and knowing far more about rock formations than any Christian insist that our world was created by an impersonal force like an explosion. Christians, however, will boldly reject the claims of the most educated scientists and insist that our world was made by a personal God (Gen. 1:1). No less authority than the Supreme Court of the United States has declared the institution of marriage to be open to homosexual unions. Christians may not have the luxury of having the adjective "supreme" in front of any of their meetings but will still declare that the institution of marriage is between a man and a woman based exclusively on the authority of God's Word (Matt. 19:5).

Many examples could be cited of using the lens of authority to clarify distinctions between common grace and the noetic effects of sin, but one example that is relevant to the concerns of many counselors is found in scientific debates about whether human beings consist of a body and a soul or are a mere body. Some scientists are strict monists and believe that human beings are nothing more than a physical body. For example,

> Nearly all of the human capacities or faculties once attributed to the soul are now seen to be functions of the brain. Localization studies— that is, finding the regional structure or distributed system in the brain responsible for such things as language, emotion, and decision making—provide especially strong motivation for saying that it is the brain that is responsible for these capacities, not some immaterial entity associated with the body.[24]

On the other hand, different scientists argue that such an approach is inconsistent with the evidence: "Empirically, scientists are faced with the data, which, strictly speaking, favor psychophysical interactionism . . . In other words, the hard empirical data are that there are two different kinds of events— mental and physiological—each of which appears to be able to affect the other."[25]

This debate between experts witnessed in these two opposite statements would suggest that Christians

24 Nancey Murphy, "Human Nature: Historical, Scientific, and Religious Issues," in *Whatever Happened to the Soul?* (Minneapolis, MN: Fortress Press, 1999), 1.

25 John Cooper, *Body, Soul, & Life Everlasting: Biblical Anthropology and Monism-Dualism Debate*. Updated edition. (Grand Rapids, MI: Zondervan, 2000), 207. Bob Kellemen cites these resources and many others in his paper, Robert W. Kellemen, "A Biblical Counseling Perspective on Neuroscience and the Soul: The 'Ghost in the Machine'—A Ghost Christians Need Not Fear," (Presentation at The Evangelical Theological Society Annual Meeting, Washington D.C., November 15, 2006), 5.

should use the lens of analysis, let scientists and other leaders hash out the data, and make an informed decision once authorities have spoken more fully to that matter. That instinct, however, would be incorrect. The Bible is overwhelmingly clear about the existence of an immaterial soul in every human being.[26] The clarity of biblical teaching on this subject demands that Christians use the lens of authority, declare that the Bible has the final say on the existence of the soul, and reject any self-styled expert with a divergent view.

Such a strong position on this issue requires that we address one other matter before leaving an evaluation of the lens of authority. That matter has to do with an issue of Christian interaction with science that has long been a source of criticism from the unbelieving world toward Christians. That issue is the debate between Christians and the scientific community over whether the solar system is geocentric or heliocentric.

For centuries, Christians believed that the sun rotated around the earth based on the purported authority of Bible texts like Psalm 113:3, "From the rising of the sun to its setting, the name of the LORD is to be praised!" Then, in the sixteenth century, a man named Nicolaus Copernicus proposed an astronomical theory that suggested the sun did not rotate around the earth, but the earth rotated around the sun. Many Christians viewed this theory as a violation of the authority of Scripture and fought back against the Copernican Revolution. This, of course, was a terrible error.

26 See my discussion in Heath Lambert, *A Theology of Biblical Counseling*, 191-201.

What was at stake in the debate, however, was not the authority of Scripture but the human interpretation of Scripture. The definition of biblical authority above is clear that the Bible is authoritative on everything *it teaches*. Biblical authority does not extend to the mistaken understandings that sinful people bring to Scripture. Human beings experiencing the noetic effects of sin are more than capable of misunderstanding the teaching of a text that maintains its true authority in spite of human misunderstanding and misapplication.

As a matter of fact, a passage like Psalm 113:3, with its language of a rising and setting sun, is not teaching anything as technically scientific as geocentricism. Instead, it is using phenomenological language to describe things as they appear. The issue of biblical authority at stake in the passage is not how the cosmos operates but is, rather, the person to whom everyone in the cosmos must give glory.

The painful lesson of this embarrassing historical example is that the noetic effects of sin remain in the lives of Christians who are interpreting the Bible. Being a member of the people of God is no guarantee against misunderstanding Scripture. When Christians apply the authoritative lens of evaluation, they must be sure that their interpretations of Scripture are accurate.

All of this brings us back to Julia and to the question of what we will say to her. What resources will we use to inform our counsel and to help with her trouble? How will we navigate the thorny issues of sin and grace in deciding which resources to use? How will we decide whether to use Scripture or some other set of resources in helping her? This is the subject of the next chapter.

3

Common Grace and Integration

Julia's story is a tragic one. In a world shattered by sin, none of us has a perfect home, but for most of us, that imperfection does not include a yearslong pattern of rape from our father living a double life as a pastor. Her tragic story created a decades-long contagion of pain that she struggled with deep into adulthood, that she carried into her own marriage, and agonized over in parenting. Every Christian wants to see Jesus redeem her story.

One of the problems we must confront in this book is that there has been a significant change over time in how effective many Christians believe the Bible to be in helping Julia. For most of Christian history, the instinct to look to resources outside Scripture did not exist. An historical shift has taken place away from helping struggling people by using Scripture toward helping people by using psychology. The doctrine of common grace is at the center of that shift.

Some have argued that the existence of common grace requires counselors to use the findings of secular psychology in an effort to care for people struggling with counseling related problems.[27] The

27 See Eric Johnson, *Foundations for Soul Care: A Christian Psychology Proposal* (Downers Grove, IL: InterVarsity Press, 2007), 113. Johnson is uncomfortable with the phrase common grace and seeks to rename it creation grace. Strictly speaking, there is nothing wrong with this nomenclature, but since "common grace" is the term used by every theologian in the Reformation, we will not

argument makes sense because we have seen how God's great love leads Him to extend grace to all people, which overcomes some of the consequences of the fall and allows us to live in a world where we can experience many wonderful things. To reject this grace is to engage in a thankless rejection of God Himself. Since counselors have an ethical obligation to offer the best care possible, then it makes sense that we would use the helpful counseling interventions exposed to us by God's common grace. Though this argument makes a certain kind of logical sense, it is actually quite problematic. To understand the problems it poses, it is important to understand the history that got us to the place where some people see the twisted sense of the argument but are blind to the problems it creates.

The Sad Shift from Scripture to Psychology

Sigmund Freud is one of the most towering figures in modern Western civilization. For over a century, he has cast one of the longest shadows in the field of counseling, effectively giving birth to the modern field of psychology and defining much of its principles and practices even today. It is absolutely impossible to envision the current field of counseling without his remarkable influence.

Freud's work began with a profound frustration. In the late nineteenth century, he was working in a field informed by confessing Christians and dominated

seek a change. See also Stanton L. Jones, *Psychology: A Student's Guide* (Wheaton, IL: Crossway, 2014), 89; Nate Brooks, "Herman Bavinck, Patron Saint of Biblical Counselors: How an Old Dutch Theologian Helps Us Make Sense of Biblical Sufficiency."

by faithful pastors. For centuries, people struggling with all manner of life's problems required pastors or other religious professionals to help them with their difficulties. Pastors understood this to be a crucial part of their labor, and books informing this practice were regularly published.

Freud was a secular man who did not like the theological definition of the counseling field and longed to be part of a change away from it. He wrote a book called *The Question of Lay Analysis,* in which he imagined a day when the counseling field would not be dominated by religious leaders, but by people he referred to as "Secular Pastoral Workers."[28] This phrase is amazing in itself. In a day before the language of "counseling" entered the vernacular, Freud described his project as an effort to do what pastors do, only without the trappings of religion and faith in Jesus Christ. He wanted *pastoral* workers to be *secular*.

To say that Freud was successful would be to say dramatically too little. It is more accurate to acknowledge that he completely redefined the counseling landscape and changed the world. When Freud began his work in the late 1800s, it was impossible for most people to imagine counseling care without the help of pastors and other religious professionals. By the middle of the 1900s, it was impossible for most people to imagine receiving counseling care from any pastor at all. Freud was single-handedly responsible for a remarkable and tragic shift in the way entire generations would think about how to receive help for their problems in living.

28 Sigmund Freud, *The Question of Lay Analysis* (New York, NY: Norton & Company, 1950), 104.

Freud's dramatic success was only one part in the shifting attitudes from Scripture to psychology. While Freud's influence was spreading outside the church, another force was spreading inside the church. That force was theological liberalism. In 1859, Charles Darwin published his groundbreaking work, *On the Origin of Species*.[29] This work was crucial for several reasons, but, most fundamentally, for Christians, it claimed scientific evidence to challenge the account of creation in the book of Genesis. Religious people in the late 1800s had never had such robust, purportedly scientific reasons to question the view of human origins presented in the first book of the Bible. When a rival account was presented by Darwin with the trappings of scholarly credibility, many Christians floundered.

The publication of Darwin's book created a shockwave of doubt concerning other teachings in Scripture. If we are uncertain about the teachings in the very first chapter of the Bible, many wondered, how could certainty ever exist about the other teachings in Scripture? Can we trust other narratives that purport to be historical? Are the biblical accounts of miracles reliable? Is the virgin birth and resurrection of Jesus true?

By the early 1900s, American Christianity had divided into two basic groups. There were the fundamentalists who held fast to biblical teaching, believing the truths which were fundamental to the faith. On the other side were the modernists. These theological liberals sought to reinterpret the truths of Scripture in order to modernize the Bible so that

29 Charles Darwin, *On the Origin of Species* (New York, NY: Penguin Group, 2009).

its teachings would make sense in a new world that, supposedly, knew better than to believe in the fantastical accounts presented in Scripture.

This liberal shift away from belief in the Bible had devastating consequences for pastoral care in modernist churches. These liberal churches were full of people who needed counseling care, and the obvious question was, "Would the cure of souls be guided by tradition or the sciences?"[30] Liberal churches who had already compromised the Bible's teaching on theology quickly moved to compromise it on ministry as well. Liberals doing their work in theology based on a secular approach to science began to do ministry in the same way. It was an approach that was as consistent as it was tragic.

The liberal shift away from belief in the Bible also had devastating consequences for counseling in churches that remained conservative, though the rationale for the changes were different. The problem in conservative churches was that the intellectual effort to defend against liberalism took all of the institutional energy away from counseling. In a world where the modernist controversy posed an existential threat to the church, conservative Christians marshaled all their forces to address liberal critiques. Students in conservative Bible Colleges and Seminaries began to receive all their education in strictly theological disciplines designed to counter the liberal threat while ministerial disciplines were neglected. Pastors were placed in churches with degrees hanging on the wall declaring, in essence,

30 E. Brooks Holified, *A History of Pastoral Care in America: From Salvation to Self-Realization* (Nashville, TN: Abingdon Press, 1983), 202.

that they had been trained in the fundamentals of the faith but not in the fundamentals of ministry. When troubled people began to seek their pastoral care, untrained pastors sought assistance from the growing field of psychology, which promised help for struggling people.[31] And thus, for very different reasons, psychology began to inform counseling and pastoral care inside liberal and conservative churches.

Integration in the Church

To use the findings of secular psychology in the counseling care of troubled individuals eventually became the default position in American churches. This project came to be called integration as counselors sought to integrate the findings of psychology with the truth of God's Word. The idea was that psychology as a people-helping profession could serve as a necessary adjunct to the teachings of Scripture, which were valuable but limited. This view has remained the dominant Christian position for decades.

But in the middle of the twentieth century, a movement began to grow which pushed back against this received norm. That movement began with the work of Jay Adams, his founding of The Christian Counseling and Educational Foundation, and his publication of *Competent to Counsel.*[32]

That movement, known as biblical counseling,

31 See also Heath Lambert, *The Biblical Counseling Movement After Adams* (Wheaton, IL: Crossway, 2012), 30-31; Holifield, *A History of Pastoral Care in America: From Salvation to Self-Realization,* 210-21.

32 Jay E. Adams, *Competent to Counsel: Introduction to Nouthetic Counseling* (Grand Rapids, MI: Zondervan, 1970).

has spread from very humble beginnings to become a global movement with committed individuals, churches, training centers, seminaries, journals, and conferences existing all over the world. The fundamental claim of the movement has been articulated well by David Powlison:

> What is a genuinely biblical view of the problems of the human soul and the procedures of ministering grace? Such a view must establish a number of things. First, we must ask, does Scripture give us the materials and call to construct something that might fairly be called "systematic biblical counseling"? In fact, we do have the goods for a coherent and comprehensive practical theology of face-to-face ministry. Scripture is dense with explanations, with instructions, with implications. We have much work to do to understand and to articulate the biblical "model." But we don't have to make it up or borrow from models that others have made up as ways to explain people.[33]

Powlison believed that Christians had the goods for a coherent and comprehensive counseling model. This conviction has been shared by every faithful member of the biblical counseling movement from

---

33 David Powlison, "The Sufficiency of Scripture to Diagnose and Cure Souls," *The Journal of Biblical Counseling* 23, no. 2 (2005): 2-14., 2-3. It is also worth noting in a book on common grace that multiple key leaders in the movement have believed that biblical counseling is necessarily presuppositional and Van Tilian. Both Adams and Powlison have believed this to be the case. See Adams, *Competent to Counsel*, xxi. See also David Powlison, "Business Ethics, Pastoral Searches, and Van Til as Biblical Counselor," accessed July 2023, https://reformedforum.org/podcasts/ctc173/.

its founding until today.

As long as integration was the default position in the church, it could maintain its dominance without any theological justification. Once the biblical counseling movement mounted a credible intellectual defense, it became essential for integrationists to ground their practice in some kind of doctrinal argumentation. For decades, the central argument of integrationists in favor of using secular wisdom for counseling was grounded in an understanding of the two modes of revelation. It was argued that God has not only revealed Himself in the special revelation of Scripture but in general revelation found in the created order:

> All truth is certainly God's truth. The doctrine of general revelation provided warrant for going beyond the propositional revelation of Scripture into the secular world of scientific study expecting to find true and usable concepts.[34]

This argument for integration had a crucial failing.

The integrationists who made this argument failed to understand the theological concepts they were employing. General revelation cannot constitute an argument to integrate the findings of secular psychology with the special revelation in the

34 Larry Crabb, *Effective Biblical Counseling: A Model for Helping Caring Christians Become Capable Counselors* (Grand Rapids, MI: Zondervan, 1977), 36. See also John D. Carter and Bruce Narramore, *The Integration of Psychology and Theology: An Introduction* (Grand Rapids, MI: Zondervan, 1979); Gary R. Collins, *The Rebuilding of Psychology: An Integration of Psychology and Christianity* (Carol Stream, IL: Tyndale, 1977).

Bible. The biblical doctrine of general revelation is not a reference to the content of all knowledge in the world. The doctrine of general revelation is found in places like Romans 1:18-23 and teaches that God reveals *Himself* throughout all creation. General revelation is not, then, all the true things that exist in the world but what God reveals about *Himself* in all those true things. General revelation is not a defense for facts in general, but rather, an argument that those facts declare the existence of the God who made them.

Those in the biblical counseling movement have known of the intellectual failure behind this argument for decades and have often made it clear.[35] The integrationist error has been acknowledged by Eric Johnson, defending his view of Christian Psychology when he said,

> Christian theologians have understood the term "general revelation" to refer to God's on-going revelation of *himself* through the created order (Rom. 1:20-23) and not the activities of humankind . . . The major problem with labeling psychology "general revelation" is it implies that the texts of psychology and the Bible are both products of the direct activity of God . . . But God's activity with respect to psychology is not directly causal; he does not inspire psychology research or texts [emphasis original].[36]

Johnson's words here correct a decades-long error

35 Just one place where I discuss this matter can be found in Lambert, *A Theology of Biblical Counseling*, 326-29.

36 Johnson, *Foundations for Soul Care,* 99.

but do not amount to a rejection of the project of integration.

Johnson is at pains to call himself a Christian psychologist and not an integrationist, but still wants to mine the resources of secular psychology and combine them with the truths of Scripture in an effort to help people with their counseling problems. Regardless of the label, the task of integration is still alive and well in Johnson's project. For the purposes of this book, the central importance of Johnson's work is to relocate the theological justification for the work of integration away from general revelation and to common grace. Indeed, Johnson argues that the reality of common grace requires Christians to discover and use psychology in an effort to glorify God.[37]

Johnson is defined by a much greater amount of theological sophistication than garden variety integrationists. Unfortunately, the presence of greater sophistication does not remove the presence of error from his model. In fact, deploying the doctrine of common grace as the theological foundation for integrating the principles of secular psychology with biblical truth is fraught with theological difficulties.

The Instinct to Integrate

Before exploring those difficulties in the pages ahead, we need to discuss why those with an instinct to integrate will always experience theological problems. We begin to see the answer in the account I have been sharing about the long move away from Scripture to psychology in helping peo-

37 Ibid., 115.

ple with their counseling problems. That sad shift did not begin with a desire to honor Scripture, but with discouragement over the contents of Scripture when it came to the practical concerns of counseling. That shift was aided by a fascination about the resources for help that exist in the field of secular psychology. The instinct to integrate is fueled by a Darwinian frustration with the contents of Scripture and a Freudian fascination with the contents of psychology.

Regardless of the label they give their system, any counselor with an instinct to integrate is part of a movement that did not begin with theological faithfulness, but with theological error. The project of integration began as psychology and was brought into the church through a combination of theological error and theological neglect. This heritage of error and neglect has persisted for decades with various attempts at theological defense which fall short for a very significant reason.

The instinct to integrate is based on an unproven assumption that the Bible is not a comprehensive resource for counseling care.[38] Doug Bookman makes a serious and, so far unanswered, charge that integrationists have focused on how to integrate Scripture and psychology before proving that such an integration is possible. "Christian integrationists owe it to themselves, to their colleagues, to their patients, and to their Lord to produce a cogent and exegetically sound rationale for the impulse [to integrate] *before* they proceed to the matter of

38 Douglas Bookman, "The Scriptures and Biblical Counseling" in *Introduction to Biblical Counseling: A Basic Guide to the Principles and Practices of Counseling,* eds. John MacArthur and Wayne Mack (Nashville, TN: W Publishing Group, 1994), 93.

method" [emphasis original].[39]

On the opposite side of the coin, biblical counselors have declared in unison that the Bible claims to be a comprehensive manual for counseling when it repeatedly says things like, "His divine power has granted to us all things that pertain to life and godliness, through the knowledge of him who called us to his own glory and excellence" (2 Peter 1:3). This claim is as bold as it is basic to biblical counseling. Powlison explains,

> Scripture is about understanding and helping people. The scope of Scripture's sufficiency includes those face-to-face relationships that our culture labels "counseling" or "psychotherapy." The content? The problems, needs, and struggles of real people—right down to the details— must be rationally explained by the categories, which the Bible teaches us to understand human life.[40]

Biblical counselors have also been clear that this bold claim is not a simplistic one. Ed Welch explains,

> Biblical Counseling is built on a simple, enduring principle: the triune God has spoken to us through the Scripture. Furthermore, through biblical history, doctrine, law codes, poetry, and songs, God has revealed to us everything we need to know about Him, about ourselves and about the world around us (2 Pet. 1:3) . . . Of

39 Ibid., 94.

40 Powlison, "The Sufficiency of Scripture to Diagnose and Cure Souls," 2.

course, the Bible doesn't speak to each of these problems as would an encyclopedia. It doesn't offer techniques for change that look like they came out of a cookbook. But through prayerful meditation on Scripture and a willingness to receive theological guidance from each other, we find that the biblical teaching on creation, the fall, and redemption, provide specific, useful insight into all the issues of life.[41]

Biblical counselors have made clear, consistent, theologically coherent arguments that the Bible is about the real problems of real people in this real world—that it is the stuff of counseling.

The events I have shared in this chapter will make discerning Christians concerned before they reach over their Bibles for other resources that the world believes offer care to Julia and others like her. Using the doctrine of common grace as a theological defense for utilizing resources outside Scripture is a new and troubling development in the history of pastoral care. So, how do we really help Julia, and what can we learn from common grace about that important task? The answers to these questions come in our final chapter.

41 Edward T. Welch, "What Is Biblical Counseling, Anyway?" *Journal of Biblical Counseling* 16, no. 1 (1997): 3.

4

Common Grace and Counseling

For three chapters, I have been stringing you along about Julia's profound difficulties and promising that an understanding of common grace has everything to do with what we would say to her and how we would help chart a course toward help, hope, and change. In this chapter, I am going to make good on that promise.

As we consider what we will say to Julia, I want to remind you of one of the books we considered in chapter two. The book is *The Body Keeps the Score*. It is no wonder that the book was an early result on my Google search—it is incredibly popular right now. One of the things you notice when you pay attention to secular efforts at counseling is that there is always a secular theory that is all the rage. These secular attempts at care gain lots of attention for a period of time—sometimes as brief as a few years, sometimes lasting more than a decade. The trauma-informed therapy that is the subject of *The Body Keeps the Score* is experiencing its major moment right now. Interestingly, the previous therapy, which garnered all the attention, drug therapy, is viewed with skepticism in this new world defined by therapy that is trauma informed.[42]

Another thing you notice when you pay attention to secular efforts at counseling is that there are always

42 Bessel van der Kolk, *The Body Keeps the Score*, 26-29, 36-38.

Christians who are lured and enticed by the therapy *du jour*. As we saw in the last chapter, there are always Christians eager to latch on to secular resources that promise to fill the gaps supposedly left by the Bible. These practitioners ride the wave of popular appeal created by the therapy and then are unceremoniously let down when the theory disappoints, and everybody moves on to the next thing that tries to succeed where the previous intervention failed.

Today we are seeing this old cycle play out with trauma-informed therapy. It is new, cutting-edge, and supposedly has much to add to the deficits of Scripture. What is more, some Christians are using the doctrine of common grace we have been unpacking in this book as the theological justification for embracing this new theory with all the promise it offers.

Nate Brooks finds in the doctrine of common grace a rationale for the use of secular trauma care in helping people like Julia. He says,

> There are helpful trauma-informed practices that don't appear in Scripture, yet we know to be true and effective from practice and research. The Bible doesn't explain how rhythmic breathing calms us during spikes of anxiety. It doesn't address grounding exercises, like holding an ice cube, to engage our senses rather than disassociate from our emotion. And there's no chapter and verse telling us how exercise can curb depression and lethargy.[43]

43 Nate Brooks, "The Bible Keeps Record of Trauma. But Is It Trauma Informed?", accessed July 27, 2023, https://www.christianitytoday.com/ct/2022/november-web-only/bible-trauma-informed-christian-counselor.html.

Brooks's basic point is that there are limitations in the content of Scripture when it comes to helping people like Julia with their trauma. These limitations are overcome, according to Brooks, in the secular resources of trauma care. Brooks argues, in short, that the doctrine of common grace gives us confidence that secular resources are more trauma informed than God's Word.[44]

But there really is no reason to get too excited about the resources of secular counseling in helping people like Julia with their troubles. On the contrary, there is every reason to privilege Scripture as the resource that corners the market on help for people like her. In this chapter, we will consider several reasons why.

Counseling and
The Higher Order of Existence

We saw earlier that, though we see the fruit of common grace and the results of sin in a fallen world, those two realities operate disproportionately depending on whether they are working on a higher plane of human living or a lower plane. The lower plane of human living involves the earthly elements that have more directly to do with this present life, like growing vegetables, paying your taxes, and solving math equations. In this lower order, the effects of

44 See Nate Brooks, "Herman Bavinck, Patron Saint of Biblical Counselors: How an Old Dutch Theologian Helps Us Make Sense of Biblical Sufficiency." "Bavinck opens the door to learning from unbelievers in those aspects of counseling that 'appertain to this earthly life.'" The examples he cites here refer to OCD, interviewing people and interpreting their problems, and wise financial stewardship.

common grace are more strongly witnessed, and the effects of sin on human thinking are more obscured. The higher plane of human living involves the heavenly elements of life that have most directly to do with God, like worship, knowledge of holy things, and human sinfulness.

Counseling fits fundamentally in the higher, heavenly plane. Of course, counseling is about issues of practical human life lived out in this earthly plane. But counseling is always—*always*—about how those normal issues of life stretch out into the higher plane of living. Counseling is about the fundamental nature of people. It is about Who made us and why. It is about our deepest desires, our most profound struggles, and our darkest fears and frustrations. Even when counseling traffics in mundane issues like monthly budgets to help reign in out-of-control spending, Jesus Christ insists that such expenditures are windows into our hearts that either look out on to the things of earth or onto the rich expanse of the everlasting God (Matt. 6:19-21).

For Julia, this is no theoretical issue. All her struggles have to do with questions about the supposedly good God that she has heard about for decades and how He could preside over decades of wickedness that has wrecked her life. How could a man who claimed to represent God be so corrupt? Can she trust any group of Christians or any pastor ever again? Is there any way that such life-destroying pain could ever issue into a happy life? These are practical life questions to which the answer is only found in the higher order of things. The noetic effects of sin will ensure that ultimate answers will not be found in strategies involving ice cubes but in the pages of Scripture and from the mouth of Him, who is from everlasting to everlasting.

Confusion about Scripture

As I write these words, we have lived through nearly a century of efforts to persuade Christians that the Bible is not as helpful in addressing their problems as it promises to be. This instinct to integrate is one of the most heartbreaking and damaging realities I am aware of in contemporary Christianity. There are a number of realities that drive these misled Christians to mislead others. One of those realities is confused categories. Let me explain what I mean.

In the passage above, ice cubes were introduced, and the apparent effect they have to ground troubled men and women and to keep them from disassociating. What should we make of the potential help trauma therapy suggests we can find in ice cubes? Well, we can start by agreeing that no such principles exist in Scripture. I also see no reason to quibble with the claim that ice cubes could have a "grounding" effect in keeping traumatized individuals from disassociating. The problem comes when we point to a strategy like this and assume that its absence from the Bible points to a deficiency in the resources of Scripture for counseling.

Secular counselors engage in all manner of therapies that are not included in Scripture. These interventions may be harmful, relatively neutral, or may even succeed in relieving some symptoms. Whether effective or ineffective, the presence of these interventions has nothing to do with whether God offers solutions in His Word that are different from and superior to what unbelievers have developed. It is fallacious and unfair to attempt to prove the insufficiency of biblical resources by pointing to outside strategies not included in Scripture.

Nothing about the existence of approaches outside Scripture does anything to erode the sufficient resources in Scripture. Brooks demonstrates a misunderstanding of this reality when he says of the Bible that

> It does not tell us everything about trauma care. This isn't a knock against the sufficiency of Scripture. There are many things that are true and important and helpful—the sky is blue, we smile when we're happy—that don't come up in its pages.[45]

Several realities about this statement demand clarification. First, Brooks claims that the Bible does not tell us everything about trauma care. If he means that the Bible does not speak to trauma the same way that recent efforts at trauma therapy do, then his statement is certainly correct. But if Brooks means, as he appears to mean, that there are gaps in the Bible's teaching about pain and trauma, which are filled by secular trauma therapy, then his statement is in error.[46]

---

45 Brooks, "The Bible Keeps Record of Trauma. But Is It Trauma Informed?"

46 Brooks seems to intend this second meaning when he says in the very next sentence, "The Bible was not written to be a comprehensive guide to all human functioning." A few sentences later, he claims, "Scripture is not the only resource God desires us to consult to understand our hurts and how we may heal." Brooks, "The Bible Keeps Record of Trauma. But Is It Trauma Informed?"

Second, Brooks claims that this alleged deficit of information "isn't a knock against the sufficiency of Scripture." On the contrary, the very careful arguments of the biblical counseling movement, made over decades and summarized too briefly in the last chapter, have made clear that the sufficiency of Scripture for counseling means that Scripture addresses counseling-related problems to such an extent that no other resources are required for counseling content. Powlison describes biblical counselors as those who believe in

> The sufficiency of Scripture for informing and defining counseling ministry because resources internal to the Christian faith are comprehensively about what counseling is about. Scripture is sufficient, not in that it is exhaustive, containing all knowledge, but in that it rightly aligns a coherent and comprehensive system of counseling that is radically at odds with every a-theistic model.[47]

Brooks is free to embrace this position or to reject it, but his argument is not the same one biblical counselors have made throughout a half-century of careful work.

Third, as evidence of the incorrect claim about the sufficiency of Scripture, Brooks employs two examples of statements that do not appear in its pages, namely, the sky is blue, and we smile when we are happy. In this statement exists one error and

47 David Powlison, "Questions at the Crossroads" in *Care for the Soul: Exploring the Intersection of Psychology & Theology*, eds. Mark R. McMinn and Timothy R. Phillips (Downers Grove, IL: Inter-Varsity Press, 2001), 33.

two confusions. The error is that the Bible actually does teach that we smile when we are happy (Ps. 39:13; Prov. 31:25). The lesson here is that we all must be careful before we assume we know what information the Bible contains. Still, Brooks's larger point remains—the Bible is not a repository for all information. That leads to the two confusions.

The first confusion is a misunderstanding between the Bible as a *sufficient* word and an *exhaustive* word. Everyone in the biblical counseling movement has argued that the Bible contains every word we need to know for counseling. I am aware of no person in the biblical counseling movement who has argued that the Bible contains every word about every topic.

The second confusion in Brooks's assertion has to do with the nature of Scripture's sufficiency. The biblical counseling movement argues that the Bible tells us everything we need to know for counseling, not that it tells us everything that may be of interest to us.

Helping Julia requires thinking in clear categories. Numerous areas of potential confusion exist: you can get confused believing the existence of outside information undermines the resources in Scripture; you can get confused about whether Scripture is sufficient or exhaustive; and you can get confused about information that fascinates you versus information that is truly necessary for counseling. Faithfulness in this area requires trusting God and believing that He gives His people the resources they need to help them with their problems in living. A great deal of information exists out there in the big wide world, but if it is not in the Bible, then you do not need it for counseling.

The Use of the Analytical Lens

One of the things that almost always happens to overeager Christians enticed by the popular counseling theory of the day is that they focus all their attention on the secular system they like and fail to see the secular criticism that comes at that system from people more expert than they. Years ago, advocates for the sufficiency of Scripture in counseling were excoriated for expressing concerns about psychoactive drugs and the media-reported panacea they were supposed to be. Such excoriation came almost exclusively from Christians who accused those committed to biblical counseling of being simplistic, anti-science, or opposed to caring for the physical body. Notably, there was little critique from the secular academic community, who knew of the limitations of biological psychiatry long before many Christians got the memo.[48]

The same thing is happening today with research into trauma-informed therapy. Just when many Christians are getting really excited about the therapy, many in secular psychology are raising serious questions about the ability of these interventions

48 See Peter D. Kramer, *Listening to Prozac: The Landmark Book about Antidepressants and the Remaking of the Self;* Irving Kirsch, *The Emperor's New Drugs: Exploding the Antidepressant Myth;* Allen Frances, *Saving Normal: An Insider's Revolt against Out-of-Control Psychiatric Diagnosis, DSM-5, Big Pharma, and the Medicalization of Ordinary Life;* Thomas Szasz, *The Myth of Mental Illness: Foundations of a Theory of Personal Conduct;* Herb Kutchins and Stuart A. Kirk, *Making Us Crazy: DSM: The Psychiatric Bible and the Creation of Mental Disorders;* Paula Caplan, *They Say You're Crazy: The World's Most Powerful Psychiatrists Decide Who's Normal;* Daniel Carlat, *Unhinged: The Trouble with Psychiatry—A Doctor's Revelations about a Profession in Crisis.*

to provide real relief to troubled people.[49] As it is in many areas of Christian living, so it is in counseling—Christians tend to be perpetually behind the times and jump on bandwagons just as the wheels are coming off.

I am not saying there are no common grace elements in the discoveries of trauma-informed experts. There are many. The point I am making is that, right now, the people with greater training than anyone who is likely to read this book are sorting things out using the lens of analysis. By the time they are done, realities that people are the most excited about right now will prove disappointing. And, when the dust settles, there will be a shiny new system replacing trauma-informed care. Everyone will then get excited about that new system—for a while. But the Bible will still be here.

The Use of the Authoritative Lens

Earlier, I discussed the doctrine of the authority of Scripture and said it meant that the Bible has the ultimate and final word on every matter it teaches. Scripture speaks with authority on every topic it addresses. The claim of the biblical counseling movement for a half century has been that, in the pages of Scripture, God speaks to the same topics that are the subject of counseling conversations.

Any counseling conversation with Julia that will have a shot at help must address the goodness of

49 Just one example is found in, Grant J. Devilly, Jeffrey M. Lohr, Bunmi O. Olatunji, "Threats to Evidence-Based Treatment of Trauma: Professional Issues and Implications," accessed July 27, 2023, https://journals.sagepub.com/doi/10.1177/026975800801500204.

God in a sinful world, God's ability to comfort us in our pain, God's power to use pain for our good, the nature of a community of faith and how it can provide care to those struggling with pain—just to name a few things. These topics are not only what Julia needs for counseling, but are the very heart and soul of God's Word in Scripture.

This reality means that Christians are required to submit to the authority of God's Word and tell Julia the words God thinks she needs to hear. Thanks to common grace, the world has access to a lot of information, but the information God believes Julia needs is included in His Word and requires the grace of Jesus Christ. The issue here is not about whether common grace allows truth to be discovered in the world out there but whether the noetic effects of sin will work a distorting effect on God's children, blinding them to the authority of His Word on matters central to Julia's life.

Integration

Since the middle of the last century, integrationists have been defined by a frustration with their under-standing of the limits of Scripture and a fascination with their perception of the wonders of psychology. Their fascination typically focuses on a new secular intervention that soon fades, and they justify this fascination with faithful-sounding arguments like honoring general revelation or embracing common grace. But it really always is the same thing. The new arguments, which use the doctrine of common grace to justify integration, are simply old-school integra-tion. We have seen it before. The enthusiasm of those with an instinct to integrate says more about their low view of Scripture's relevance for trouble than it does about the actual contents of Scripture.

That is a word of rebuke and I want to be careful. We are living in a nasty world that too often hands out insults, abuse, and offenses. I do not wish to be part of the coarsening of our culture. But I am also aware that in the biblical worldview, a rebuke can be a kindness, serving as a rescue from a dangerous course (1 Tim. 5:20; 2 Tim. 4:2; Titus 1:9; 2:15). With all my heart, I believe those Christians who cherish an instinct to integrate are on a dangerous course. Let me explain with a story.

Years ago, after a long day together, I was walking with my cherished mentor and friend, David Powlison. We were talking about a book that had just been published by a Christian with an instinct to integrate. As we were sharing our frustrations with the book, he winced, looked down, and said, "I really hate it for him." When I asked what he meant, he explained that the author's dismissal of the use of Scripture for counseling indicated an obvious personal problem. The author could write about the apparent limitations of Scripture for living and the glories of psychology because, though the Scriptures had glorious resources, the author had never experienced them.

In counseling, we always share the overflow of what is in our hearts (cf., Matt. 12:34). When Scripture has powerfully impacted us, we will counsel Scripture. When the resources of the world have impacted us, that is what will come out of our mouths. Powlison was right. When counselors get excited about the resources of the world, they reveal a gap in their own hearts that Scripture has not yet filled. Since you cannot give what you have not received, integrationists spread their frustration with the glories of Scripture to those they counsel and thus perpetuate the error. My heart breaks over such a situation.

Rest assured, everything is at stake in this issue. I mean that with all my heart. When we get frustrated with a perceived lack of resources in Scripture and become enamored with the latest secular therapy, we will do something very damaging to Scripture, to our souls, and to the people God gives us to help. We will begin to make the Bible seem like it is a book that is really important for teaching how to get saved but is not as important for how to live a saved life. This is a corruption of the form and purpose of Scripture. The Bible was written to be a comprehensive guide to all of human life and functioning.[50] When we step away from Scripture's resources for counseling and utilize the world's resources, we also hurt people by exchanging the Bible's lasting, powerful, and Spirit-empowered principles with more or less harmful replacements. Time in counseling is a zero-sum game. The more time we spend in counseling working with secular resources, the less time we will be able

---

50 Nate Brooks actually states the opposite: "The Bible was not written to be a comprehensive guide to all of human functioning." This statement is mistaken. The Bible is, quite obviously, a comprehensive guide to human functioning, and is the only resource under heaven that is such a comprehensive guide. Such an erroneous statement is difficult to understand. Perhaps this is another instance of confusion between the words "comprehensive" and "exhaustive." If indeed he meant that the Bible was not written to be an exhaustive guide to all of human functioning, then the statement would be true, but the value of the statement would be lost since nothing but the mind of God Himself could ever be such an exhaustive resource. Nate Brooks, "The Bible Keeps Record of Trauma. But Is It Trauma Informed?"

to spend unpacking the glorious truths of Scripture. I have counseled hundreds of people who struggled with pain and trauma, and I have never talked to one who regretted our lack of engagement with secular therapies. I am ready to promise that eternity will reveal countless counselees who would gladly trade their time engaging such therapies, regardless of any common grace value they may hold, for time spent lingering over the Word of God.

Before moving along, I need to make a comment about ice cubes. The grounding effect of ice cubes was one of the "helpful" interventions of trauma-informed therapy in the quote above. Of course, secular therapy, in general, and trauma-informed therapy, in particular, commend many other interventions beyond ice cubes. When you study the therapy, you will find they also commend many other things the Bible does not mention, like yoga,[51] acting in theatrical productions,[52] and following a therapist's finger with your eyes.[53] For those with an instinct to integrate, all of these strategies pose an equal temptation to replace the glories of Scripture with other mundane therapies. The concern of faithful biblical counselors is not whether there is any common grace value in any of these strategies. I am sure that many of them have accomplished some common grace benefit in the realm of symptom relief. The concern is whether they are worth comparing to the rich resources in Scripture, or whether they are like fading grass in comparison to the Word of God which stands forever (cf., Isa. 40:8).

51 van der Kolk, *The Body Keeps the Score,* 265-278.

52 Ibid., 336-48.

53 Ibid., 250-64.

There is no reason for this biblical frustration and secular fascination. In fact, biblical counselors believe that we must never trade biblical truth for secular resources because the Bible is full to bursting with resources to help any struggling person, regardless of the problem. Let me prove it with a brief discussion of how one passage helped Julia.

Psalm 107 and Counseling Julia

Scripture is replete with wisdom and stuffed with re- sources. Many books have been written making this case, so I do not need to say everything here. Instead of talking about the comprehensive scope of Scrip- ture, I will focus on Psalm 107 and the help just one chapter of Scripture offers someone like Julia. With everything I know about Julia and with all the infor- mation I have about Psalm 107, I could spend many months counseling Julia just from this one passage of the Bible. In this small book, we will limit ourselves to a few pages.

We will start with what we do *not* know about Psalm 107. It is one of those pesky Psalms that does not give a lot of information about its historical context. That means there is much for scholars to debate in the way of who wrote it and the situation the author was facing. The truth is, we just do not know the answer to these things. I actually like that. The anonymity of the passage gives Julia permission to make it her own, and the lack of clear context allows her to press the words of the text onto the details of her situation. Even a casual look at Psalm 107 demonstrates that the overlap between the biblical text and Julia's life is nothing short of incredible.

First, it is clear that there is no deficit in the psalmist's understanding of pain and trauma. The entire psalm is full of references to trouble (107:2, 6), distress (107:6), the longing soul (107:9), darkness (107:14), the shadow of death (107:14), destruction (107:20), being at your wits' end (107:27), oppression, evil, and sorrow (107:39). Psalm 107 is nothing if not trauma informed. When Julia encounters these things, she feels understood and heard. She is comforted by the fact that the Bible "gets" her.

Second, the Bible acknowledges pain but does not let us remain there. The psalmist gets us moving from grief to relief. In Psalm 107, there is wave upon wave of pain. But after each new crash of suffering, there is a refrain in the passage, repeated four times, "Then they cried to the LORD in their trouble, and he delivered them from their distress" (107:6, 13, 19, 28). For each new round of pain, there is a fresh grounding in truth from the ever-present Lord. Trouble is real, but God is present. Distress is cruel, but God is loving. Pain will not respond to your agony, but God hears your cries, He knows your pain, and He delivers you from distress. God's people are grounded, not with the cold chill of an ice cube, but with the warm love of God Himself.

When God responds to these cries, He acts in objective ways that are designed to help. His activity reframes pain. His power charts a path out of the darkness. The psalmist knew, and now Julia knows too, that God acts to redeem from trouble (107:2), to lead in the direction of help and safety (107:7), to bring satisfaction in a longing soul (107:9). God delivers from the dark shadow of death (107:14);

He breaks the bonds that hold us in our suffering (107:14); He heals old wounds and delivers from present pain (107:20); He silences the screeching storms of suffering (107:29); and He brings all of us to a haven of rest and safety (107:30). God does all these things and more. But for Julia, the most help and comfort came in the last thing God is described as doing in Psalm 107.

God talks about Julia and everyone like her as those who are "diminished and brought low through oppression, evil, and sorrow" (107:39). Those words describe the details of Julia's wrecked childhood and the lingering pain of her spoiled adulthood. But God's Word does much more than give language to past pain, it charts the course forward into the future of what He is doing to redeem her life. The psalmist says of God that "He pours contempt on princes and makes them wander in trackless wastes" (107:40). This passage tells the truth about what God thinks of Julia's father, who was perceived as a "prince" of a man by all who did not know the truth as she did. The truth is that a righteous and loving God has nothing in common with such vile perversion. Instead, God will pour out judgment on this wicked man. And Julia? God is going to direct all of His love and all of His power to turn every ounce of evil for good in her life. She will see it and be glad, "[God] raises up the needy out of affliction and makes their families like flocks. The upright see it and are glad" (107:41-42).

These glorious truths have everything to do with another fourfold refrain throughout Psalm 107. It is the repeated cry of those afflicted people who have been delivered from their pain by a great and gracious God: "Let them thank the LORD for his steadfast love, for his wondrous works to the children of man" (107:8, 15, 21, 31)! Julia has a bright future in store, of seeing with her own eyes and experiencing in her own heart the steadfast love of God. When she experiences it, she will have a heart full of gratitude that will pour out praise for all God did.

This is an incredibly brief example of the richness that exists in Scripture to understand and reshape our brokenness and trauma. It is just one psalm, and there is much more in it that we have not touched on in these few words. Even a brief survey reveals that the richness and authority of even one passage of Scripture is not worth abandoning for any outside source. Christians should celebrate any common grace intervention that God has given to relieve pain and difficulty in a truly hard world.[54] But a desire to offer real and lasting care demands the admission that it is secular resources, not scriptural resources, that are deficient to offer true help. Common grace requires the addition of special grace to offer real care, not the other way around.

54 In this chapter, I am making a strong case that the resources of common grace should not be used to provide the content and strategy of biblical counseling, regardless of how much we might celebrate that common grace in other areas of life. For more information on why our celebration of common grace does not require the usage of common grace elements in counseling, see Heath Lambert, *A Theology of Biblical Counseling*, 65-101.

Concluding Thoughts on
Common Grace, Counseling, and Julia
••

Common grace is true and wonderful. If anything, these words are an understatement. Because common grace makes it possible to eat, drink, breathe clean air, and avoid the unmitigated consequences of human sin, it makes life possible. Because common grace is behind every medical advance, every beautiful song, each exquisite portrait, and every wonderful novel, it makes life beautiful. You and I simply could not enjoy life or exist at all without God's unmerited favor lavished on the human race in common grace.

As wonderful and important as common grace is, it does have limitations. We have seen that the effects of sin are not completely eradicated by common grace. Instead, we live in a complicated world with the tension that exists between humanity's universal sinfulness and God's common grace. In this muddled world, human beings get some things right, some things wrong, they mix other things up, and figuring out the difference is often harder than it first seems.

Common grace, while of great value, is also not ultimate. The ultimate display of God's grace is found in His special grace, where He extends eternal salvation to all who have faith in His perfect Son, Jesus Christ. This reality makes common grace the servant of special grace. The strongest advocates of common grace have known this to be true. Bavinck declared, "Common grace is indeed subservient to special grace."[55] Kuyper proclaimed, "Regeneration yields a distinct epistemological difference that ultimately

---

55 Herman Bavinck, *Reformed Dogmatics: Holy Spirit, Church, and New Creation,* vol. 4, 470.

leads Christians to interpret reality differently (and with better precision) than that of non-Christians."[56] The particular grace of God occupies a lofty place of precision in this world that the subservient common grace simply does not.

Common grace serves special grace as it focuses on ultimate realities but common grace is not itself focused on those same realities. This truth is of profound relevance in a book about common grace and counseling because, while common grace is not about ultimate realities, the discipline of counseling is. Counseling is focused on problems we experience in this life which require special grace for their solution. Those solutions are only found in the contents of Scripture. This is a fact that biblical counselors embrace and that everyone with an instinct to integrate denies.

It is neither a lack of knowledge of common grace, nor a failure to appreciate it that leads biblical counselors to reject the use of secular psychology in counseling. The rejection is because biblical counselors believe in biblical authority and know it is that divine authority alone that addresses the ultimate issues on the table in counseling. Biblical counselors avoid psychology in counseling because they believe in the love of God, that would never give His people a final authority that was not also a sufficient authority.

Integrators, with their uneasy relationship to faithful theology, are lately pointing to the old truth of common grace as the new defense for their distrust

56 Abraham Kuyper, *Wisdom and Wonder: Common Grace in Science & Art* (Grand Rapids, MI: Christian's Library Press, 2011), 25. See also Louis Berkhof, *Systematic Theology*, 439–40; and Van Til, *Common Grace and the Gospel*, 13.

of the Bible as God's resource to care for His people when trauma and trouble strike. It is important to be clear that any disagreement is not about the reality and celebration of common grace. The disagreement is about whether it is possible to trade the things of heaven for the things of earth when it comes to counseling troubled people.

Common grace supplies so many things in counseling it is impossible to count them: it supplies education so that people can think, read, and speak clearly. It provides craftsmanship for everything from the building you are meeting in, to the chair you sit on. It supplies everything as mundane as the coffee you might drink during your meeting to something as important as restraining the sinful will of a counselee who does not want help but comes for counseling in spite of himself. It provides the phone system you used to set up the meeting, the pen and paper you used for the notes, and the binding on the text block of the Bible you are using. Common grace supplies all these things and more, but it never takes center stage. Common grace never stops being a servant. Common grace does not and cannot supply the strategy for or the content of counseling conversations. That role is reserved for special grace, and the Holy Scriptures are alone sufficient for that.

The sufficiency of Scripture for counseling is not a euphemism for "simplistic," "easy," or "uncomplicated." Mining the Scriptures for God's sufficient wisdom is at least as hard as mining secular material—it just happens to be more fruitful. Biblical sufficiency does not mean that it is easy to figure out how to help a person with complex problems, that every person using those sufficient Scriptures is equally skillful, or that the content of the Bible is arranged the same way secular resources are. God has His own way of organizing His system. It is ours to study, pray, and seek wisdom, not to throw up our hands and retreat to other resources we judge to be superior.

The only time common grace will play a central role in counseling is in the counseling practice of those who have never experienced the inward renewal of God's special grace. Darkened to the glorious resources of Scripture, such people will have to grope in the darkness for any light they can find. But if you have made it this far in this book, you know that the noetic effects of sin will ensure that light is not the only thing they will find in their stumblings. They will encounter much darkness too. Every faithful Christian must lament the poverty of resources secular persons have in their attempt at solving the serious problems that plague broken people. No Christian should ever consider reaching across a closed Bible, with its wealth of resources, to hand their counselee an ice cube.

All of that brings us back to Julia and how to care for her. She was not in need of secular approaches to help or of dubious theological defenses for such approaches. She needed real help. She needed lasting care. And that is what our congregation gave her. At our church, we were able to help Julia to resolve her difficulties and to help her live in the light of truth (or, if you like, to be grounded and avoid dissociation). We were able to do all this without recourse to new therapies that sell lots of books. All of our interventions came straight from the pages of Scripture. By God's grace Julia changed, and if you tried to use a theological-sounding argument to make it seem like the Bible that changed her life was lacking in resources to help her, I honestly do not know whether she would laugh or be offended. But, standing on the hope and peace she now enjoys, I know she would never believe you.

Questions

1. Why is it so important to believe the doctrine of common grace?
2. Why does the doctrine of human sinfulness make it hard to discern the existence of common grace in specific instances?
3. What do the lenses of assumption, analysis, and authority have to do with counseling?
4. What does the doctrine of general revelation and common grace have in common with those who seek to integrate biblical truth with secular psychology?
5. How is it that biblical counselors can value common grace without using its discoveries in counseling?

Bibliography

Adams, Jay E. *Competent to Counsel: Introduction to Nouthetic Counseling.* Grand Rapids, MI: Zondervan, 1970.

Bavinck, Herman. "Common Grace." In *Calvin Theological Journal.* Grand Rapids, MI: Calvin Theological Seminary, 1989. 51.

_____. *Reformed Dogmatics: Holy Spirit, Church, and New Creation.* Vol. 4. Grand Rapids, MI: Baker Academic, 2008.

Berkhof, Louis. *Systematic Theology.* Grand Rapids, MI: Eerdmans, 1932.

Bookman, Douglas. "The Scriptures and Biblical Counseling." In *Introduction to Biblical Counseling: A Basic Guide to the Principles and Practices of Counseling.* Edited By John MacArthur and Wayne Mack. Nashville, TN: W Publishing Group, 1994.

Brooks, Nate. "The Bible Keeps Record of Trauma. But Is It Trauma Informed?" Accessed July 27, 2023. https://www.christianitytoday.com/ct/2022/november-web-only/bible-trauma-informed-christian-counselor.html.

_____. "Herman Bavinck, Patron Saint of Biblical Counselors: How an Old Dutch Theologian Helps Us Make Sense of Biblical Sufficiency." Accessed July 27, 2023. https://rts.edu/resources/herman-bavinck-patron-saint-of-biblical-counselors/.

Calvin, John. *Institutes of the Christian Religion.* Grand Rapids, MI: Eerdmans, 1989.

Carter, John D. and Bruce Narramore. *The Integration of Psychology and Theology: An Introduction.* Grand Rapids, MI: Zondervan, 1979.

Collins, Gary R. *The Rebuilding of Psychology: An Integration of Psychology and Christianity.* Carol Stream, IL: Tyndale, 1977.

Cooper, John. *Body, Soul, & Life Everlasting: Biblical Anthropology and Monism-Dualism Debate.* Updated edition. Grand Rapids, MI: Zondervan, 2000.

Crabb, Larry. *Effective Biblical Counseling: A Model for Helping Caring Christians Become Capable Counselors.* Grand Rapids, MI: Zondervan, 1977.

Darwin, Charles. *On the Origin of Species.* New York, NY: Penguin Group, 2009.

Devilly, Grant J., Jeffrey M. Lohr, and Bunmi O. Olatunji,. "Threats to Evidence-Based Treatment of Trauma: Professional Issues and Implications." Accessed July 27, 2023. https://journals.sagepub.com/doi/10.1177/026975800801500204.

Fox, Margalit. "Dr. Peter J. Jannetta. Pioneering Neurosurgeon on Facial Pain, Dies at 84." Accessed July 26, 2023. https://www.nytimes.com/2016/04/15/science/dr-peter-j-jannetta-a-pioneer-in-neurosurgery-dies-at-84.html.

Freud, Sigmund. *The Question of Lay Analysis*. New York, NY: Norton & Company, 1950.

Holified, E. Brooks. *A History of Pastoral Care in America: From Salvation to Self-Realization*. Nashville, TN: Abingdon Press, 1983.

Johnson, Eric. *Foundations for Soul Care: A Christian Psychology Proposal*. Downers Grove, IL: InterVarsity Press, 2007.

Jones, Stanton L. *Psychology: A Student's Guide*. Wheaton, IL: Crossway, 2014.

Kellemen, Robert W. "A Biblical Counseling Perspective on Neuroscience and the Soul: The 'Ghost in the Machine'—A Ghost Christians Need Not Fear." Presentation at The Evangelical Theological Society Annual Meeting. Washington, D.C. November 15, 2006.

Kuyper, Abraham. *Wisdom and Wonder: Common Grace in Science & Art*. Grand Rapids, MI: Christian's Library Press, 2011.

Lambert, Heath. *A Theology of Biblical Counseling: The Doctrinal Foundations of Counseling Ministry*. Grand Rapids, MI: Zondervan, 2016.

_____. *The Biblical Counseling Movement After Adams*. Wheaton, IL: Crossway, 2012.

Murphy, Nancey. "Human Nature: Historical, Scientific, and Religious Issues." In *Whatever Happened to the Soul?* Minneapolis, MN: Fortress Press, 1999.

Murray, John. "Common Grace." In *Collected Writings of John Murray*. Vol. 2. Edinburgh: Banner of Truth, 1982.

Peale, Norman Vincent. *The Power of Positive Thinking*. New York, NY: Touchstone, 1952.

Powlison, David. "Business Ethics, Pastoral Searches, and Van Til as Biblical Counselor." Accessed July 2023. https://reformedforum.org/podcasts/ctc173/.

_____. "Questions at the Crossroads." In *Care for the Soul: Exploring the Intersection of Psychology & Theology*. Edited by Mark R. McMinn and Timothy R. Phillips. Downers Grove, IL: InterVarsity Press, 2001.

_____. "The Sufficiency of Scripture to Diagnose and Cure Souls." *The Journal of Biblical Counseling* 23, no. 2, 2005.

van der Kolk, Bessel. *The Body Keeps the Score*. New York, NY: Penguin Random House, 2014.

Van Til, Cornelius. *Common Grace and the Gospel*. Phillipsburg, NJ: P&R Publishing, 2015.

Welch, Edward T. "What Is Biblical Counseling, Anyway?" *The Journal of Biblical Counseling* 16, no. 1, 1997.

About the Author

Dr. Heath Lambert has been preaching at First Baptist Church of Jacksonville, Florida, since January 2016, and became Senior Pastor in September 2017. Serving First Baptist is the joy of Pastor Heath's life. He is delighted to serve with the remarkable members and staff at this incredible church. Prior to serving at First Baptist, Pastor Heath served as the Executive Director of the Association of Certified Biblical Counselors (ACBC), and as a professor at The Southern Baptist Theological Seminary.

Heath earned a bachelor of arts (BA) in biblical and theological studies and political science from Gordon College in 2002, a master of divinity (MDiv) in Christian Ministry from Southern Seminary in 2005, and a doctorate (PhD) in biblical counseling and systematic theology from Southern Seminary in 2009.

He is married to Lauren and they have three children: Carson, Chloe, and Connor.

About Shepherd Press Publications

They are gospel driven.
They are heart focused.
They are life changing.

Our Invitation to You

We passionately believe that what we are publishing can be of benefit to you, your family, your friends, and your work colleagues. So we are inviting you to join our online mailing list so that we may reach out to you with news about our latest and forthcoming publications, and with special offers.

Visit:

www.shepherdpress.com/newsletter

and provide your name and email address